Aloada's SHI T FACTORY

Aloada's SHI T FACTORY

Aloada's Shirt Factory

A Christmas story: Exploring the adventures of Prickly Pole.

Aloada's Shirt Factory is a grown-up Christmas story for the child in you, and yes, me too.

Introduction.

It's time to take your medication, dear, she said to her husband lying on the bed over there. "Almost dead?"

"No, he wasn't really sick, as you might have thought and said, about it." But they were newlyweds, so...

She... she'd just given it to him, yes, the book she'd found amongst her things. She'd gotten him to agree to do it in bits and pieces over tea, didn't have the time to do it all in one sitting line, you see. Even though it was small, they were newlyweds, after all. Since they'd fished it out of the medicine kit, they would have gotten the hunch; let's do it in dosage, short and quick. Over lunch would be a perfect practice. Or on any other of such normal habits, just like biscuits to crunch, but... "Oh sheet!" That was it, daily dosage to fit... That was it, this is day no. 1; so the story began.

"*So, you wanted something different and unique? This is it. It's not your typical "Girl meets boy, winning the joy, character-hopping, plot-wrapping, sweetie-flick bit." This is Aloada's Shirt Factory, and it's Prickly Pole's story. Yes, it's a story to go, because it's short. A Christmas tale to warm your heart.*"

This story is told from a Carib-Jamericanadian perspective. In a richly blended language-mix of nonsense talk, sensational spelling, double entendre, poetry, and seasoned with snippets of Jamaican Patois inserted here and there throughout, as may be found fitting. Yeah, man, a Jamaica yaad mi come fram, sorry, I meant to say; I'm Jamaican born and bred, okay? Yes, wordplay is the order of the day around here.

1

Day One

The Newlyweds

Look, that's the shirt factory right there. Yes, Aloada's Shirt Factory is just across the way from where he prays for some helpful beings to come someday. To usher him into his home of abode, his habitation down the road, one might say. But it never came; that help still remains somewhere out there on the fertile plain.

Prick and his mother, Mrs. Long, live on the ground floor of the same building sin ting, or is it something? "Yeah, say it that way, okay?" "Good." The basement apartment is reeling him in. The prick man is headed there right about now, hunched over the arguing cow. Arguing yet more about the pole, and complaining about how he's stuck with dragging it between his legs and up near the hole where his right riding hand is firm on the hold. His favorite horse-and-jockey position from way back in the days of old. Even though he (himself) isn't that old to be shaking cold in his soul. But. He's been doing the stick-riding thing from way back when he was just another child about the children's playpen. "What!" "Yes, he's almost alone here in the frigid zone and riding again. But he ain't... I mean, isn't. He isn't having fun at it none. Not like he used to, no. Not at this time." But really now, tell me. What if you should find out that the thing that you thought you were seeing was not what it is in reality, Hingh, and wasn't what you were really seeing? Because it's not what it really is made out to be?

Like, Kiss me. Kiss me nuh. Kiss mi nuh man. Kiss mi damn teeth, kiss mi granny one teeth. Yeah, *"the lucky tooth." Seeit yah.* Look at it.

He was stuck to the pole, halfway between the shoulder and the sole. You know, the sole of the foot and the shoe. He would, of old, p... P hiss up against it, yes, up against the stick. Or at least, act the part of doing the sort. So, whenever it was convenient for him. Or even when it was not, you know, like, when it was not convenient at all! He would pull for the bull, and the full length of the tool. He wasn't known as a "Prickly pole" yet when it got settled on him and started, but things weren't turning out as they'd wanted. Born in the tropics, he was just like any other of the jackets about the pit. Just like any other bouncing baby boy. Beautiful was he, like a mother's joy tree. There was nothing to indicate that he would have to wait with a skin issue to meet up with his fate, and the misuse. But as he grew, it began to show. Showing up for him and you, "no?"

"No."

"Okay then, I'll go." By the time he was ten. He was all covered over in them. Then comes the running, hiding, abiding, and covering up to try to cover it up inside him. You know, like, to cover up the shame. He stood out from the crowd from very early, and very loud, too, was the slashing of the sword, Leigh. For all the wrong reasons in a crowd, most assuredly. Over there in that square, they called him spikes, or even spikey, sometimes, and that was because of the skin condition, unsightly, friend of mine. Come to think of it, I've heard them say that you've got a skin condition of your own, too. Is that true? You do, do...? Do you have a skin condition, in truth? Like, the swelling type? No? Okay, I hear what you say, but. What's that? What did you just say? It's not about you? Yeah, I hear you. Well, goodnight, boo-boo.

He's right, though. We're talking about the spike show, yeah, man! You're right, too. We're talking about Spikey Prick here, not you. Anyway, as the young boy grew, he became more and more reclusive. By his teen years, he was hiding and abiding behind a lot of clothing to suit me, in their... In the tropics? Not a good topic to get things fixed and to fit in with the "Mode." Not a good combination of code, no. Not a good thing for a young boy in any condition, Hingh, let alone in a tropical setting. His mother had to get him help or get him out of there. The latter came when he was seventeen years of age.

2

Day Two

Walking Hunched in A Winter Wonderland

Memrie and Olivine Long, mother and son. Look, their time has finally come. They'd arrived in the winter wonderland way up north. The longer ones, both Olivine and Memrie, took to the new environment there like fish to water sent out to sea. Some of the time, yes. But the winter wonderland has a way of getting very summery some of the time for Memrie. He was to find this out and had to adapt quickly, or else. "He else it." Since he couldn't adapt quickly enough, yes, that's why he did the "else" part. Splitting the seasons of the year into two halves as it suited him and his "special needs" conditions spots. He loved the winter conditions as well as the opportunity they afforded him; he was to become Santa Claus, in-house Santa at the shirt Factory, in its proper, applause. Aloada's Shirt Factory, that is, and there at the factory is where the other stories were developed, like a battery. Rather quickly and to his glory. He avoids the outdoors in the summer, though, avoiding it as if it were a plague foe.

He was walking home by himself, yes, just him as usual. He never hangs with anyone, not even a new gal; didn't have a girlfriend or any such thing, you know. But now, "What is this thing that I'm seeing?" somebody was heard asking. "What's going on with his lumpy skin?" What's this thing now hastening in and pouncing on him and me to see?

Mr. Prickly Pole was very cold, but that wasn't all that was tugging at his soul. He opted for it and grabbed a supporting role in his... "Fist?"

DAY TWO

"Yes." Happened when he reached out and took hold of the very first and closest piece of a long thing his eyes would have seen, and which his hand was to come across. It was a pole, alright, but a metal pole, tight at last. He'd have a long history of doing that sort of mystery. Been doing things like that from way back in his story. In ancient times, he would have used a thing from the line. You know, like, a piece of a stick of some kind that was used for supporting a clothesline, like, a piece of wooded bit that wasn't mine. But, ever since his arrival here in the great white northern hemispheres, he had to quickly change that habit. Since he was having some trouble finding that sort of prop double of a stick when in the park, he would hobble and spit on all of you. You know, like, out there where he'd sometimes walk. But there's always the alternative bark to light up a spark. It appeared down there near the place where he lives; his lucky charm came seeping in through the sifting sieves. It was a pole, yes, but a metal pole test. He stuck it straight up in front of his gut because he wanted to go down to the hut. Got to do what he's got to do, you know, but... You know, it's like, like, when a man has got to go somewhere, he's got to go there, and fast. So, he couldn't wait a minute late, and could no longer wait to meet up with his date. Like, the long-overdue date with the approaching fate. He's got to go out and do what he wants so very much to do do. He was heavily under the spell of it, too. Now, straight and steady, look. Wow, help me... I mean, him. Because the pole is heavy, but he's ready. Ready to make himself less heavy by leaning it up, or more like, standing it up in front of him. He then pulled it out and placed the spout... yes, that one. The spout that was quickly out, the other pole stout, the short pole, of course. He pulled it out and then placed it behind the stick. Behind the handhold of the longer pole grip. Right there between him zipping it in and out by himself and the said metal stick, thing. The pole ring of a *sin ting*, or something. Hang on. Here it comes; here comes the longer one, running, after first wrapping up and down and all around him. He went along with that easing plan thing until it was all done. Relieved he was to become, a minute or two later on. Because it wasn't much later, *dung*... I mean, down, like, not much later down the line, when he was to find that, yes. Everything was going to be all right. Because he was going to find it, or more like, lose it, all night. He would have lost it all right there and then. Aahing away under his breathing breath, my friend, his breathing breath to stay amended, it felt sooo... good.

3

Day Three

Stranger in the Night

At the same time, look, look at the other guy. Mister Stranger, yes, him, not I, but. Yes, it was Stranger Coward, I think that's what they call him, or some other such "something" soured, wink-wink. He was coming. Approaching the intersection, humming. He hummed his way in from the opposite direction to play. A stranger saw him coming that day. Or did he? Well, maybe not, if one should go by the way he was to react.

"I could have sworn that I saw that guy walking towards me," he said. No, he ain't lying, mi Bred... I saw him coming towards us, so he might have seen him too. Coming off the reel and rolling into view. He was walking up a moment ago. Coming straight towards me, and you, and him, that same Stranger Cowardly thing. Along with everybody else walking along the Constantly Springing Boulevard. Approaching from the opposite direction, all by themselves and heading towards...

"I was mistaken," said the strange one. "It seems as if I'm imagining things," said the same stranger once again, under his "Steamy breath." "Or, is it a dream yet?"

"No, not at all because he did say so." It's obvious that the guy is there doing his thing, like, working the beam. He's just doing his part of the job thing. He's a surveyor, holding up the pole stayer for his neighbor partner. Look, Stranger is scratching his head now, and turning around to watch out for the surrounding sound, and yet more such sounds were coming down and slowing down to a complete stop as he was "looking around." To the left, and then to the right of him. Then over there near the nook, well-lit and bright to cook him, I think. He's scratching again, a little bit confused, is his name. Or a lot, you know, like, a lot confused again. "Where's the other one? His partner in the plan? Where's he?" He was asking everybody now and again while looking at me as if I were to be blamed for her... yes, she... "Where's he?" He asked himself, seemingly, not knowing his name. Usually, there are two of them, one for the pole and the other for the real machines, for the goal. You know, like, the tool that they use to get the job done. The real equipment for the task at hand. The cameraman at last, *yeah man*, that one. Or whatever else it is that those people may use on the task, in order to get the job done fast. Or even slow, like, slowing it down to push up costs on our ask in parts as they used to do in the past. Now, look, look at him fast, and be sure to also look at the evidence, as he is there pocketing the lump sum that you and I, the taxpayers, would have lost, in their defense. But he's looking around him, still, and behind him, *just chill*. Stranger knows that he's there too, somewhere out there beyond the blue. "But where, I wonder!" Is this what I think it is, though? Or no, but wait a minute, could it be... No, it can't be. But why? Why is he behaving like that, P? Why that strange look about him? Why is he so overly focused on his frontal attacking spree to spin? Look at that. A lot of handling seems to be going on in that spot. And what's going on with that thing about his demeanor ring? That scary, airy look that's now impacting him? "Am I missing out on something here?" Asked he, yes him, as I was to overhear.

"Heard, the word is; overheard."

"Okay, Mr. Shepard." Well, not anymore, though, my dear, I swear, I won't be missing much more from this point on, and in. So said the same Stranger man, yes, him.

4

Day Four

The Candy Man Can.

The camera was there, hanging on its holder and dangling down from the long string on the shoulder, before. Stranger's shoulder, that is, and more. Yes, more things were hanging by the glue there in the offering gear, that's true, my dear. And yet more than that, too. Other things were hanging there by the long string, stretching across the chest and the back of his vest. It was like, like, everywhere. Whichever end of the staring one might catch a glimpse of him from, the back or the front of the man. It was there and hanging on, got the hunch yet?

"Yes, but not anymore, though. I gave it away; no need to sweat."

"I know, now stare, or, in other common words we use out here, 'look.' Let's take a closer look in there." Stranger is prepared to engage the gear, and yet more than that, is he, don't ignore the degree, okay? He's preparing to do something, just like me, yes.

"Like what, to go to work?"

"Well, probably, perhaps it's too jerky; chicken. Shooting something, maybe. Shooting the pole man, perhaps, and whatever else might be going on, on the worksite, let's see." He might get lucky and win something plucky. Like, capturing whatever he can to get stuffy when stuffed into the can, with me, now look, he's about to shoot. Oh no, not the candy man, that brute, is not that cute. But as for the cameraman? He can surely do that kind of canning, of whatever is going on therein. Yeah, in there, with the camera, my dear, yes, that's with what? You thought he was going to shoot him with a pistol dart shot? No, Chrystal

Smart, it's not that, seen enough p-hissing sort, sorry, I meant to say, pistol sorts of things since the rise of the morning. Seen enough of that kind already for one day's daily bread. No, don't yawn, Hingh, no p-hissing pistol, please stay, don't go, please stay, don't. Go away, yes, now. Anyway.

Stranger has got to capture the scene. He's going to need some real hard dough bread to go. I mean, hardcore evidence, to show, real hard evidence of it, you know. Of what he thinks is going on here and there, and thence. Or not going on in defense of the trench somewhere near the peripheral fence. Depending on what side of the storm one may be looking at, and seeing things from. The missing of things from this point on and in... will be missing in action, Hingh. Not anymore, he's now quite sure, but you know. He's sure of this and that; he won't be missing the list a lot. Even though he didn't know what the list was before this, he knew enough to have known that he could not afford to miss this one thing that he would have hissed upon to pis..., I mean, to kiss.

"Is it really something?" I overheard him asking. He thinks it might turn out to be "quite interesting," well, so he said, to himself and them. Yeah! Quite good, as a matter of "actual fox skin." It felt so good. Like I, even though I'm now thinking thoughts that it could just as easily be naught. But that's what he said to his felt hat through the fraught. But as for him and her, blur. Look, he's focusing now and shooting the cow. Recording it all for the record-keeping and storage, Hingh, how... At the same time, watch the sign, here comes Jonny P. You know him already, no?

"No."

"Well, John, public is he, but you didn't hear it from me. Now look, he's rolling on in." Yes, that guy's skin is, as you'd guessed. John Public and everybody else with him in the goblet are passing them by, not to sit. But they're going on down to the bar to go drink up some friendly brew, and spit. He's having all his friends with him. They're seeing these things, but not necessarily because they're looking at him. It's nothing at all to them. "Nothing to see here," someone was heard saying to him, my friendly dear. It was just an occasional stare, called working gear to amend something, out there. Just a couple of surveyor guys serving up the layers' eye. Going about their business, like real players, not I, doing the job a favor. Look, one is holding up the pole, straight and steady, the other is shooting — "What, shooting the job already?"

"No, no violence in here, Freddy. It's not that type of shooting anyway, my dear. But more like, capturing the gear." He wanted to capture whatever is out there happening, anything that might need to be captured, since you're asking. But in reality, Mister Pole, the prickly, that prickly pole guy, look at him quickly. It's he who is holding up the pole and shooting, too. All at once came the screw, no?

"No, oh no, screwing was not something he was accustomed to coming over here and doing." So said the nosey neighbor who was dropping in on things that didn't belong to her, you, or him. He's right, though; he'd not gotten near enough to the peripheries in those spheres yet to be doing the screwing. Nor to be joining you in doing that sort of friendly brew, Hingh. Prick never did get that far as to be stirring the stew pot, no. But seeing things from another point of view is what he'll do a lot of. From another direction, and from the use of another piece of high-priced equipment, too. *Who knew?* How the tables have now turned on you. Now it's the pole that is holding the holder, and he, the Prick, he ain't liking it one bit. "*Woah, mei shoulder, it ah hat mei.*" There's a sharp, hurting feeling in my shoulder region; the direct aftereffect of over-exposure to too much laughter this season, but...

5

Day Five

Riding Again Today
 Look, it's Aloada's Shi t Factory. It's just across the way from the Pottery. Yeah, that street right there, where the flowers are in full bloom and so very pretty to eat. But they must be plastic because the air is still nippy out there on the street, and looking on and over the paths. But won't obey the commands to go away to taw. Actually, I must not forget to say it properly. And by the way, that's a SHIRT factory right there, across the Pottery-Bey. It's surely in need of some repair, no?

"No."

"Okay, whatever you say, that signboard is really ripe and ready for a repair job already, though, for it to be steady." It's there, the shirt factory, along with all of the other garment manufacturing entities in the building. This is the very building that collectively supplies shirts and other garments of worth to the Shirt Depot for packaging, argument, and distribution, as sent to me. It's the largest of the entities in the building that helps her pay the rent properly. Prick and his mother live on the other floor of the same building sin Ting. Or something. Yeah, that one. The basement apartment is reeling him in. The prick is headed there right about now, hunched over the argument cow. And arguing yet more about the pole and how he's dragging it between his feet and moving on up to the flat, cold, to a deluxe old apartment near the hole. His favorite horse and jockey position from way back when... Like, from way outside of the cold, and from in the days of old. Even though he himself is not that old to be shaking cold in his soul. He's been doing it, though, yes, he's been doing the stick riding thing bit from long ago, way back when. You know, like, from when he was just another child going about the children's playpen. But he's almost alone here in the frigid-zone rain, and riding again, horseback bare. But he ain't having fun none. Not like he used to do over there in his old hometown. Not this time around. Oh no, my dear. But really now. One has got to ask it a time or two more. What if that thing that you thought you were seeing wasn't what it was to be, Hingh? Like, wasn't what you were actually seeing? Because it was not what it really was, B Hingh? *Kiss me. Kiss me nuh. Kiss mi damn teeth.*

6
Day Six

Welcome to My Door
   Here are some other adventures of the prickly pole that you might want to stuff in your dresser drawer. He had to drag the pole inside through a hole in his bid to get out of the cold. Well, it was the regular old hole through which he had dragged it. As well as himself, and flogged it, and everything else. He would drag everything inside the building through that hole. The hole through which he and everyone else would have gone in every time, to get out of the cold. Well, so I was told when I wasn't lying... down. It's called a doorway sign, down home. I think. Or some other such thing.
   "Not to drink, though?"
   "No, or was it, well... No more guessing, about his address. It really was on the doorway type of a hole, way. What a mess!" "..."
   That doorway, though, might be "regular" alright. But not so much so on this night. There was nothing regular about the way he'd entered that hole and the building where he shared an apartment with his mother, who paid the rent. No, not this time, nothing regular about it at all, Mass Vincent Ross, and you, too, Clementine. According to the tell-tale sign upon the welcome call. He was hunched over the pole. The metal pole that was wedged up there between his leggings, heading up near the bowl. While he played the part of the jockey riding the mount towards the finish line, or the finishing pole, to post his time. See the sign? Yes, he was going in there to go sign in, to go do the stunt. Whichever of those terms you may fancy her the most, while on the

winner's hunt. Onlookers seemed to find it very funny, laughing away. Mission accomplished one way or another, one might say. Well, that's part of the mission at the very least, Kishon. But boy oh boy, if they only knew the agony, agony, agony, and the pain that he was encountering, while they were there laughing off their latter ends, at him. They probably would not have been all that jolly laughing away Miss Molly's day. But...

7

Day Seven

The Remedy
He was about to discover that the hot water remedy brew that his dear mother and the lady had suggested and thrown through... And would have gone in and prepared it for him, too, wouldn't do. She was trying to administer it to his... I mean, to him, but it was the wrong thing to bring. It was the wrong call. Couldn't have been wronger at all, her. "Couldn't have been more wrong" was going to be the new song in town.

Wtf. What murderous tormenting effects it was beginning to have on the already overly sensitive pod? Like, the skin scab he would have grabbed and bagged on the jag over from the West Indies cod. Now made worse by cold freezing. Frozen seeds such as these are never to be squeezed, Hingh. Such deeds he surely doesn't need. He should have paid far more attention to the pleas and the many often-told stories. Like those stories that he would have been hearing since the time of his arrival here in the early days of glory. You know, like, upon his arrival in the winter wonderland spheres of snow. Stories such as those he was told, some funny old gold, really. Stories of mischievous kids, Neily. Daredevil kind of kids, even. Children who would have gotten their tongue stuck onto a cold, old, metal pole, rotten, in the deep zero degrees temperature-ZZ, below freezing-eee. Easy *nuh*, man, please. He never did, though, never did he listen to much of those things. "That's their kind of story," he'd said, not too reassuringly mi bredrine, "not mine." He would have thought it silly most of the time. Up until Willy would have hopped on in and latched himself onto the filly, and... He was to have feely, I mean. Did he not feel it? Really? Now, though, he's finding himself stuck tightly to a cold old metal pole spikily. Somebody strike me, please, and oh, how he wishes it was by way of the tongue, man, *goh siddung*. Sit, doodle, sit. Good dog. Yeah! Look, look at him, I'm patting him down, hard.

8

Day Eight

Mr. Long Was a Good Man, But...

Phil Forbes was clearly a square, but everyone knows, not so gentle a man was he. He lives and reigns in the upper echelon of the societal spheres, you see. Up there is where he belongs, but not for much longer, to be... As things now stand, he and his clan will soon be gone. But as for Mr. Long? Listen on, Mr. Long and his family are still living over there on his farm, along with all of the other indentured workers and servants. That, however, wasn't the only family that Mister Long had. He was too clever for his own good, perhaps. He had a family before that, whom he adored a lot. But he left them over there, on the other shore, and who, for the most part, isn't there anymore. They have all moved on, too, to the great white northern hemispheric view. Way over there, beyond the pointy-finger peer through. Well, at least two. Two of them did. They had to get up and leave. Mrs. Long and the kid, the prickly pole kid.

Mr. Long was a good man. Well, he still is, but not as seen through the eyes of everyone. Certainly not in the same way as how Olivine sees things when it comes to him, yes, when it comes to "that man," as she now takes to calling him, from time to time. It was the job that he didn't have that would have caused him to leave the home pod, to go down to the South American farm, rowing a rod... You know? Like, to work hard at sending back the money that the young family needs and wants to get along like every other growing family, planned... But then, upon his arrival there in the southern hemisphere. Well, it was really north of where he was coming from to appear in those years. After having run headlong into those vivacious dancing long-haired girls singing the songs. Somebody was going to change his worldly plans. Nothing has been the same since. Olivine would have lost her charming prince. Mister Long is just like a lot of the other indentured workers who live there on Phil's farming acres of the squares. But from the looks of things, the Phil clan will soon be gone, over to Singh's, perhaps.

Phil is now an old man, and the sons he wanted and would have had only amounted to one, and he, as it now stands, isn't much of a man. Well, as seen through his father's eye, in disappointment, and looking on. At first, there were two, and both of them were some sort of "Hugh." In somewhat of a sense, screwed. First, let's talk about that one. There was Hughstand, he who came in running after Hugo. And they did just that in a sense; Hughstand stayed standing on the farm, very put there under the sand. Or lying down. Yeah, that one. He died and is buried there, even though he was the youngest of the two Squares: Hugo, though, left the place and went, yes, man, he went away. Actually, he was sent away to go to school and do university, so they say. In a land far away, a country-pool sort of stay to learn how to swim and play, came home not quite the man he used to be. Well, at least not in his father's eyes to see, and he? He himself hasn't been able to remain quite himself and stable since either. The vile one, as it stands, seemed to have placed a scalding hot kiss upon the old man's lips, and his heart just flew away with it. His mind was quick to follow, too, hastening on to obey whatever you tell him to do. Sit, sit, yes, that's it. So now, it's not just one but two of them, two individuals who used to be men. At least one of them was thinking that way. He was thinking of himself as being so, they say. Would have thought it was the same with his suntanned children, too, today. But what's left of them now isn't much to see the plow, both of them. Both the father and the son are to be found walking around down home, and as numb as headless, mindless clowns. Such a pity, just when things were looking really pretty. Not just for him and his family, but for everybody who works there on his property, but... back to the prickly. Back to that dust.

9

Day Nine

Christmas is A-coming, and...

So now, it's just about Christmas time, coming on *dung*, down the line, and his Christmas gig at the depot crib? It's gone big-time, *fa nung*. Yes, as of now, it's all gone from him, and oh, how, of course. He hopes that it's going to be just a temporary setback, of a king spree. No longer than that to be, and for many more reasons than the lot to see. Seeing that he will soon be well enough to get back on track, back there, and will be as good as new, come next year. Way before next year comes along to appear too, as a matter of fact. Hey, you! Yes, you there, be sure to hear this clearly. Make no mistake about it. Yeah, Leigh. That would be great for sure, don't you think? Like, if he should be back and as good as new in a wink? "True?"

"True."

But for the time being, a substitute will have to do, suffice it to say, because. Unless you or anyone else is flirting with trouble. Can't have a couple of rambunctious little kids double-bouncing around to play in those quarters in and around the waist in deeds way. Or a whole bunch of them, even. That's no way to stay in those bays to play, as is the custom. Or even worse, like having a bunch of them hanging bids out there at the Depot crib without Santa on Christmas Eve, no, *goh cuss dem*, I mean, go curse her, on these. But it's even worse than that, as bad as the thing has already gotten a lot. Can't have them hanging their bids out on it. Like, hanging those bids out on his laptop atop his... Nor bouncing around there on the spot somewhere near his pair of pittance of gear, you know! His pair of knee-pants, yes, that's what we're here talking about, my dear aunt, Aunt Tess. Nor anywhere in proximity to that place where the nitty-gritty had long promised him that the next rocking stage show would be. In the present state of the Bulge area, to see. No, not that kind of bulger. Don't you get it too vulgar, you twisted mad as Foskor. Oats, yes, get out and come back in through the doors against the post mess. Now, the thing for you to quit is this, the argument, because Iris... As was first trusted, that thing is done, busted, bruised, and blistered already as it is, mister. Cruise. Padded up and bandaged and put upon the sandwich. All hanged-up upon his bedded down sticky carriage, and leaning upon the arms of his mother's advice sausage sawed off his... The other half was handed off to someone else to do, do... Off the one that was handed down to him beside the bowl of porridge, as given to you. Since nobody but nobody must ever venture in and around that region of the prized hillside possession except for her and him. Mister Prickly pole and his thing, them only, and only because of the current class in session. That's the only reason his mother would have had a welcoming season and have a welcome mat put out at the door spot. Not even that welcoming anymore at that, but as said before...

10

Day Ten

Language Test

On this fact, she was enabled to enter and act on the peripheries of the stable on such hallowed grounds and lots near the stable. It was the one thing that would have afforded Mommy Veenie to enter anywhere near that promised land, by all accounts and indications. That's how it has always been up until then. Yes, yes, mei fren, my friend really knew him then. Up to this point in the plan, even. There might have been some other folks, though, who, in recent times, too, might have poked pointed spokes around your toes, and around him and you, you know. Like, toying with grandiose ideas and dreams of changing that situation at the station, soon. Maybe someday in a darkened bedroom. Or on a solemn occasion, such as Christmas morning, coming on down soon, just for instance. Someday in the not-too-distant future, I'd say, not to be too incensed, and salute her hides, okay? As it is now, though. It's coming on Christmas Eve, slowly. Will someone be getting lucky, please? Like, this year? Pleaser? Just wait right there and stare. You never know what you might get to see popping up here and there, and everywhere else, please "s." Like, please excuse me for making a massive mess of the Queen's rather charming and beautiful language test, cute e? But you know me, not that bright, you see. This rocky road, though, may yet lead somewhere slow. Like, somewhere better than here. Or there, or anywhere else. Anywhere other than where roads had led Prickly pole so far this and every other year. Yes, yes, Mister Mistar. There. What now? What do we make of those two women, his newly found wannabe female friends? Or at least one of them, one of the two. Like, the one who had been trying to befriend him for all of that time in... you know who... The one who had been going at it the most, like, from god knows when and who but. But who still have not been able to penetrate the line through the brick wall that he, the Prick, tall, dark, and handsomely handyman like me sometimes is he... like whenever he's in the mood. Prick can be pretty good when he's in the right mood, which is hardly ever good. In the mud, probably "H*ey, clever.*" In "The Mood," though, it can be quite another story to savor, so... But he has been handy at building things into the wood, even out of it, properly good. Well, so it would seem sometimes, Mr. Woods. Like walls and stalls, for example. Some of which will soon be decking the hall, man, that place is a sample. All the rest of the "building mess" with which he sometimes messes around at his address, too. Like the brick wall that he had been putting up, tall and tranquil between them and you, Mr. McAnuff. Like, in between himself and all of them, the women folks, most of all, my friend, are just as good, and—"And everyone else to call?"

"No, no, Paul. That's as much 'all' as you may need to install to fill up the stall." So, what now, Paul? What's going to befall? Like, now that the metal pole, tall, has been added to the brick wall? A blessing or a curse? Or nothing at all, Nurse?

11

Day Eleven

Frozen Solids

Zero degrees temperature, "What places are these?" He was asking her. So now, like his... balls... point, the pen has frozen up wither, again. Oh! Please. Yet stuck up again some more is the door to the very same one you know. The pen is what we're talking about, Hugo, right?

"Right."

"Yes." The one he'd planned on leaving in his will and test for testing the testament tonight, is locked up and secured, tight. Left as a legacy handed down to his children, and to their children's children after them, right?

Right. But now he's beginning to doubt if it will ever pan out and happen, after what would have happened to him. They saw him there, barely walking; he was walking sort of funny through the square, but they didn't really care, like, as to what the reason was. But there, look, look at it again, yes. You can see it all if you will just stop and look. As seen through the looking-back memory lens of this nook, seen? "Seen."

Yes, they're turning around to book the cook, yes, man. This one is a big-time chef in this neck of the "Nook." Come on. So, there they go, looking all over the brook, Lyn, and laughing. Laugh as much as you like. Your day is certainly coming, ma-hite, or going, to be bright. "Right." You just need to wait. Coming next, the prickly pole song, to sing along.

Here's the Prickly Pole song.

Oh boy, prickly Prickly prickly pole, poor boy prickly, prickly Prickly pole. Got himself, got himself, got himself stuck to a pole, stuck to a cold old metal pole. It's cold out on Christmas Eve.

Oh boy, prickly Prickly Prickly pole, poor boy prickly prickly Prickly pole. Got himself, got himself, got himself stuck to a pole; stuck on a cold old metal pole. He's whole on Christmas morning.

Come, one fairy whose palm was hairy. Sliding down through the mirror since there was no home chimney –*scary*. But when next he woke up. His mom was in the room, *as usual*. With the bowl and a spoon —*as usual*— cooking and cleaning from morn till noon—*as usual*— but, but, but again. Woke up whole. Prickly pole, woke up whole. Woke up whole, or was he?

Solo.

It was on a painy Christmas morn, Christmas morn, Christmas morning. He woke up in the Morn... and yawning—*yawning*. Cover his mouth over, and over with his... Palming... *still yawning*. To discover without so much as a warning. The poles were gone, the skin was Norm... smooth as a baby newly born, and then he too was gone, gone, stone-cold out of it again, out of each and everything. *Talking exchanges.*

"What happened?"

"He fainted!" Thought he was dead and buried, gone to heaven, and not to his bed carried. Or, someone must have gotten married. Him perhaps! Laughs. Hahaha ha ha ha haa. Well, it could have been that you know, or something. But, but. Cut.

12

Day Twelve

Don't Go, Please Stay

Now, back to the story of the day. Doctor Choux didn't know, or else he would have been up and going. You know, up to the doorstep and in through Prickly's front "Doe..." Hingh. The backhoe, too, looks... it would have gotten stuck like glue before it had gotten through the said doe. Sorry, I meant to say the doorway, to try and save them the day. They were there with him in the room in the morning. Both of them were in the dorm, and warming. His mother soonest, as usual, and her friend and wannabe girlfriend to him were to come in next, oh, you again, *my pal*! You know, like, *that gal. That gal, that gal Shelly-Ann*. Yeah, it was her. But, oh man!

"What is she doing here?" He, the Prick man, would have asked as if sworn to swear. "What are you doing here?" He was to swear again. But to the face of her this time in, standing in front of them right there behind the deadline stare, Ben. Well, more like hunched. He was hunched over the crunch in front of them.

"Get out. Get out," he was heard to shout, "get out of here."

"No baby, no, don't say that to the lady, oh no dear." Said his mother lady, there. Whilst reaching out a soft, touching hand onto "Shaky," shaking the shoulder of her baby (the big prick man, you know), to smooth out the bruised ego, maybe.

"It's, it's, it's okay," the nosy neighbor was heard trying to say, but...

"It's not okay," was the repayment coming at her by way of the same pickney, Prickly Pole. While dragging himself away, quickly. From the hold.

"It's, it's, it's alright, Ms. Long." Said the goodly good-buying woman while reaching out to get hold of the door jamb. She was sort of informal like that one when it came to Mrs. Long. Unlike how it was with everyone else with whom she gets along, all of whom call her Mrs. Long. Not so with Miss Nosey, neighborly, wrong. She seems to consider it a favor to just call her Miss Long like that. Then go save her out... by saving a lot. So, she obeyed and tactfully went away.

"I was just about to be leaving for home anyway," she was heard trying to say. "I suppose I can come back again some other day."

"No, oh no, don't you ever come back here again, ever," at the top of his lungs under the brain, he shouted the blame at her. "Never! Who let her in here anyway? How could you? How could you?" He further blamed the woman he knew. His own mother, a lady who was to be found there wearing the shoe. "How could you?" He was shouting away. All anew.

"Calm down, son, calm down."

"Don't you tell me to calm do... Aah." He said this, however much of it he would have gotten to say. He would have said it while trying to get away and get himself up off the stick bay... sorry. I meant to say, off the bed, hid down on the lit, yeah, the bed thing you know, where he had just sat him down to sit, but, oh sheet!

"Ah. Oh-eeh." Back to reality.

He was still sore there. Still sore somewhere down there in that region of the core, branded beer, yes, there. Right there where they had hung the wild, boring steer. But not so sore that he could not turn the key. Nor was he so upset in the eyeset so that he could not see. You know, that he could not see the vet, and the working wonderment in his mother's medicated eyeglasses next, but. In arguing the argument, and in her demeanor, a moment or two later. She was standing there, when she was standing up there, again. After getting back up front, and up from off her toe, near where she wasn't standing a moment ago. Because she would have been back up on her feet, you know. Up from the falling to pieces of her buttercup. Fell flat out on the hind... scout of her sin luck. You know her; she was never a saint like that buck. But then, when she was standing there, like, standing up again to stare. Or walking about the room with a puzzled look on her moon. You know, her moon-lit-up face was faced with an air of utter amazement behind her teeth brace, as it was to be seen, smiling up at him and gracing his face. Calmed down the place. Calmed him a degree or two down, too.

13

Day Thirteen

Just Got Myself Killed

Meanwhile, on some other day, while he was there, watching the scenes play out. Somebody was about to see a guy get himself killed by the side of the road, to get away. "How, but, but. How?" He got himself run over by a car. The very one he was helping to push out of a jam... jar. But he still had to get up and walk away, not even knowing that he'd just died that very day. No, I couldn't tell him that. For what? What good would it beget a brat? Never mind, though, I'll tell you some more. I'll tell you how it all went down, through the bore. Now, this is how. It was in the height of winter, or more like the lows, the sub-zero degrees to which the place is known to please. This guy would have gotten his rear-wheel-drive car stuck below the knees, in the snow, and on the ice, oh please. After several attempts at trying to power himself out again, without success. The young man, that very same young man whom we spoke about earlier on, on ends, yes. He who had been standing by and watching the happening, like the nonsense, I, I...

He then decided to lend a helping hand to him, you know, like, to the old man who was skidding... off the road. He (the young man) offered up a "helping" hand. He's that kind of man, so. He went to the rear of the car and proceeded to push forward while the elderly man applied more power to the drive train. It's known to have worked in the past, you know, even in the muddy rain. There are times, sometimes, when just that little nudge will get a vehicle out of such a situation, sludge, and to slide, or not. "No, not again." "I know." So, they would have done that for a while without success. "What a shame." At the same time, the nosy neighbor, Leigh. "The one of a kind..." No, not her this time, not the friend of the prickly one for sure, he's not going to save her the dime as an extra thing to score. But quite another nosy neighbor of a man, and more. He was sitting there at an exalted place and watching the "Happening" before. That was when he noticed the tragedy that luckily, didn't bother to happen to his newly adopted daddy anymore. The elderly man, in his attempt to get out of the jam, would have hit the gear shift lever from the forward position where it had started when it began. The young man opted to assist him by offering him a hand. He (the older one) hit the reverse position and floored the gas pedal, the piston. Then back, forward, and then reversed, and again. One two three times four, or even more, my friend. The problem is, all this was happening unbeknownst to the young helper king. He who was all the while still there and pushing in one direction, Hingh. Luckily for him, though, all that effort would have led to failure. This is one of those times when failure is the biggest success of thine. Even by a country mile west and prime. Can you imagine what would have happened if, for some strange reason, the wheel of that car had found a grip? Even while the gear was engaged in the direction of where the young man was, and pushing the ship? The prick man can, and he, maybe only he, would have been able to see. Yes, that was him there, waiting for her, not me. The other nosy neighbor, Leigh, was on the square. He got to see it all, and what he saw was this: A young man getting run over, and lying there dying in the snow, freshly fallen all. Just by trying to help out an old Foo L... of a person. Oh, sorry, I almost "out" the guy, and worsened his fall. I'm really sorry for almost revealing the guy's identity like that. What I really meant to say was an old man in need, and flat. And then, the young man would have walked away, probably thinking of himself as a failure in some way. Someone who wasn't able to help out an elderly man in need, I'd say. But not knowing even until this day, probably. Not knowing that he was successful in saving a life, pardon me. His very own life, even. Even if it's just for the pleasure of pleasing his wife in the evening. He's not going to be seen as anybody else's high-riding knight, though. "No. You'd better go — "Okay, I hear what you say, so. Go, I will, I'll go away." All that and more, though, can be found right here, wrapped up in this bundle of paper, torn to pieces and square.

14

Day Fourteen

Questions of the Day
"What is it?" He asked.

"What is what?" She mocked the reply, as if in class. You know, she was sly in the reply, yeah, that's why.

"You, you. You have this, this strange look about you. There's this, this weird thing about you this morning, what's going on in there? What's going on, Mom?"

"Nothing. It's nothing at all, eat, eat, eat up your breakfast and... and, and go back to bed. Go back and lie down, and go to sleep," she said. She then pushed the broom back in the corner and pulled the door shut behind her. Then walked back out of the room and into the gloom of the short passageway and on down, passing the bed. Then continued back in towards the kitchen tomb, carrying the tray with the things, like, like the spoons. Look, the dirty dishes and the teacup from yesterday are on the keyrings. That's where they were to be seen sitting and swinging from the morning way through to noon. She was carrying them back to the kitchen and to the sink pan, come to think and croon on, on... where she would then go back to spend twice as much time. Washing and scrubbing her thoughts and her mind of all that had happened in the room. Like, all of the perplexity that would have been uploaded and overloaded onto her thinking on this, the eve of Christmas Eve morning.

"What was that?" She wondered, a-mock, that thing that she was now seeing? Was she seeing things where none such would have been?

Was it her mind playing tricks on her, again? She'd spent what up until this point would have seemed to her like... like a whole lifetime. Wishing and hoping for a miraculous sign, such as thine, even, and, you know, she was hoping and praying too, for a miracle of some kind of hue. One that never before seemed to be forced forward to be found forthcoming through the nipple. While the baby was lying with nursing, nibbling on the feeding bottle, but now? "Could it be? Could it possibly be?" she was heard asking me. Or was it her mind playing tricks on her in this, and on me, again? But just then. The telephone rang, ringing her back to life again, brang, brang. Then back to reality, too. Just like that, and then, also ringing her back down to earth again, with you. She would have reacted uncharacteristically frightfully to the ringing telephone pole of the light... full Leigh, you know? As with a bang, of useful pulls, unusual, though it might have been, usually. It would have been delightful. But, as for this time? It was as if it was the first time that a phone was going to be ringing on her house line. Or even to be heard whining in her earring chime. It was her, calling back again as it occurred. Miss Nosy, neighborly, my friend. She'd called back to check up on the lot of them, if only to see, and inquire on the situation attached to thee. You know, to both of her friends and He...he, yes, him. Laughing. She was rather coy in her approach. Didn't want to seem too nosy a roach. Hey, you. Crush it, go crush that roach, crush it quick, then come back here to sit and listen. Yeah! That's it, now, let's get back to the stories we've been missing. A tale about Prickly, in all of his glory, mi pickney. Like, not wanting to be too pushy, yeah, that would be She... yes, her, Miss Nosy neighborly as it occurred. She would have had all the right and topical things to say upfront. After all, it was Christmas month.

15

Day Fifteen

Talk Up the Thing

Anyhow, back now to the cow, I mean, back to Miss Nosey neighbor, that's how. Look, and listen up, too. She's slanting the talk, King. Can't be coming across as too brash on the first catch — "Of plantain?" "...yes, who's asking?" Not too pushy, even worse than that. She would have had all of the right and topical things to talk about and to say upfront, and first. So as not to be talking about the hunch, in the purse. After all, it was Christmas month, and coming on the eve, after all of this. "Curse!" She was talking about the gifts she wanted to get given, oh please. But Christmas wasn't worth the call. It wasn't what she had called to talk about at all. Or even the eve. It sure was not Steve.

"She knew," Mother Longer one whispered, amused. Yes, she, Mother Long, knew all about it too. Mrs. Long knew, yes, and now everyone knows it, I guess, even you, *oh sheet*! It was him, the prick man thing, that's what, that's who. That was who she had called back to go screwing a round hole within you. I mean, to check up on, and to talk about. She'd noticed something, too, no doubt. "Prickly pole" was what they used to call him. Everyone who knew him around those parts of the town-end knew him by this name. Not only because of the poles in his veins and on the upper body game, but he seemed to have been carrying them all over him, like, on his face and upper body phylum... um. For those who may have gotten close enough to him to have seen that much of him and of them, those poley things. You know, as if it was something cooked up and oiled down, like him, the bumpy pole thing. That wasn't the sole reason, though, for the name, no. But it was partly because of the blame; they were blaming it all on where he was from. Yeah. That was the blame game for them to *nyam*. Go on, eat it, eat it, don't you let me re... no, that's all. But still, go. Go eat it up, your breakfast. Heat it up and eat it up. That's that. Now, back to the place, that spot. It was because of the place he came from, yes. That was the thing to be blamed. A place in the country of his birth and origin. A tiny hamlet of a place by that very same name, me bredren. Yes, my brother. From the first day, he would have made the mistake of telling them that he was from the Prickly Pole state. That was his name, so I was told, times 8. He wears them there on his body, too. The other poles, as we're told. He could even be covered all over by these poles, anew. They were not moles, no, they were bigger and pointier than moles, and you? *Who knew*! Nobody had managed to get close enough to him to have been able to see all of them, but his mother, perhaps. Perhaps she would have seen those spots. So, only him, and yes, her, perhaps. He and his mother alone would have seen enough to have known the extent or the full coverage of his bladder upon the malady. But the other was on the ladder, yes, the latter that she too was climbing up, to bother me. Miss Nosy neighbor knew enough, enough to get her to interfere in ringing things through the cuff, from her hair, a lot. She would have been close-up with him, like close enough before, to have been able to see the poles he wore; the gigantic bumps on the nose outside the bore. He has lived his entire life, I suppose, and as it would seem. Trying hard, I mean, trying to keep it under his clothes and out of sight. From the sunbeam, too, and shunning the lights. He's done a fairly good job so far in this regard, it would seem. Starting from home in the land of his dreams, as seen by those living in his original tropical country yard. "Oh, My Lord! Is that his home phone on the hanging cord?"

"Mi nuh knoah, but." "..."

He would have done anything whatsoever, anything that it would take to keep out of the way of what other people spoke and spake; that's what he would do, and if and when he could not avoid people, he would have lied his way through the vehicle. Found innovative ways to protect his secret issuing days, and sidestepped the gaze."

He would sometimes pp quick up against it. Up against the stick, you know. Peeping up against his pole, which he always carried in his hold. Or like, at other times, when it would seem to be carrying him whole, and wholly...

"Holy moly! That was kind of folly, and like..."

"Like what?"

"That, like," (Pointing).

"Yes, like galloping along the track down the alley, whenever he's acting the part as if he's riding a horse, yes."

"Yes, or getting ready to take off like a witch on a broomstick stalk?"

"Okay, I'll just agree with you and say, yes." That's how he would have done it in those days, his way. He would sometimes lean up against it as if he were p-hissing up against a pole or a tree. Like people used to be... People usually do it in those times and in those places.

"Probably me, no?"

"No, no 'probably' here again, Addie-Lee, that's how it was back then, literally," nothing to bother me in its traces, nothing at all. Even in biblical times and places, that was the call, yes, that was what people did. That's all. No? Well, the Bible did say so, no? Was that not what it said? Well, okay. I'm shrugging my shoulders away, on my way to bed.

16

Day Sixteen

How Are You Doing Today?
"How is he?" Those questions were coming in from her, yes, Miss Nosy, as it occurs. As in, a nosy neighborly frosey. That same no-hosey personality. "Ugh! What's that? What are you talking about?"

"Prick, that's what, that's who, how's he doing today, any better?"

"Oh, sheet!" *She whispered*. "I don't know. Really." Mummy was taken aback because. They were there chit-chatting about a lot of nothing, as a matter of fact. Like, about Santa and the sack that he carries around on his back, or something. They were to be wondering about such things, wonderful, wondering questions were tumbling in on each of them, coming from either direction of the argument as to how he was carrying those things. Or as to how he was getting himself carried in by the winds. How did he manage to get everyone their gifts in time for the Christmas morning bits of early lifts, like mine? That's what they were there to warn him... I mean, talking about, and this. To avoid talking about what they were really there to talk about. Now, hiss. Or more like who? "He's okay, I guess."

"What do you mean, you guess? Didn't you check up on him yet, like, I ah, I mean, like since, since...?"

"No, I didn't, have not gotten a chance to do that yet."

"You shouldn't be waiting for a chance to check up on him, Aunt. You need to keep a watchful eye on him at all times and... and — "And what?"

"And make sure that he is okay."

"Okay." She said, and then, look, she's walking away.

17

Day Seventeen

Standing Upon a Stan

"I'll be getting home a bit late this evening," she said to him, yes, to the man, yes, him, that would be Stan. "I'm going to look for Mrs. Long's son — Prick." That was it. She'd said this to him, to Stan, tall and hip. You know him, yes, he's the man.

"How did he manage to lose it, though?" Lied wide-eyed, Stanley Rowe. He was asking this of his dreamy-eyed future bride, the girl of his dreams, you know. She, who was busily walking away at the time, was on the go, passing him by again. Walking by fast on the other side of him.

"...And I, I don't understand, for the life of me, I cannot, and could never understand that one, a lot. If he had somehow lost it. Why then, why couldn't he go back and look for it and try to find it for himself and Margaret? Why you, my friend?"

"I'm going to see prick, Stan, you lunatic of a man. I was not talking about your brother Dick now."

"Oh, come on, leave my brother out of this one, will you? But really now... Oh! Well, of course, of course, you are, in a way." So said Stan, across the bar, with a gigantic smirk on his face, pan, pan... for, you know. Like, he was looking down at the tar. While looking sideways and down the road to avoid the gaze upon her loaded chord. He was looking everywhere but at her face. You know, he had it all there, upon his own frontal space. The smirk! No disgrace.

DAY SEVENTEEN

"I'll be here when you get back, too, just like I've always been, waiting for you. Thought you might want to know that, you know, just in case."

"Just in case of what? You're really something else, you know that, Stan? We're not talking about the same thing here, Stan. And why do they call you that anyway? Why do they call you Stan as if you're standing upon a stand when you are always sitting? Just sitting there and (apparently) doing nothing. Do you ever do anything, Stan? Other than sitting there and interfering in other people's business affairs? Man! What a man! Yeah! Some kind of a man, thing, you are, Stan!"

"No, I don't, I sure would like to be doing you... You, like, on the hunt, you know, doing something, anything at all for that matter, but you won't let me. Nobody ever lets me do anything anymore. Not you, not them. Not nobody. I mean, not anybody. You'd much rather go looking for a, ah, you know, a prick. You know, that man friend of yours. Not me, though, nor Dick, like, my brother, so go. Go right on, can't keep a prick waiting for too long, can you?"

"Bye, Stan, bye, see you soon."

Stan was the man around those parts and still is, to a certain extent, sort of and as silly as... A hotshot cop and all-around girls' man, he is, as is said about him, in regular, everyday kind of talks around those parts in the indies.

He's retired now, they say, retired from the force. But not from life, of course. Doesn't have a wife; I'm not sure if he ever got hitched at all. But why should he go around and bitch at her when he can spree and go about so carefree? Wants everything that wears a dress from the dressing room, at the address where he's messing around on the bed, down in the room where he happens to sometimes likes... or dislikes being spoon-fed into feathering the bed.

But he doesn't seem to have a problem finding and getting them, as the evidence seems to suggest. Those women? They're the best, as for her, however, and whenever it comes to Miss Nosy neighbor, Leigh. No luck there for him to favor me, it would seem, at least not yet.

18

Day Eighteen

Propping Up the Pole

Back to the pole again, to Prickly, that's the man's name. A pole was a handy little prop and a trusted friend at that, on whom he could fall back and depend a lot. "And relax too, right?" "Yes, and to sit down on you tonight." Rolling the eyes. "Too bright." It's been such to the boy since then. Like, from way back when. But that was in another time and place, way back in a tropical space in the Caribbean. The new space in the far north doesn't lend itself well to that sort of condition. The cold, old winter wonderland doesn't lend itself quite as well to being dragged around a long pole, white or brown, in hand. Especially, not a metal pole as known to the man. He was to find this out in the strangest, harshest kind of way yet. Yes, in those days and in that neck. Let's pull back the curtain now and take a peek in, just to be certain if he's in. Let's now look into that before we move on. Yes, he is, so we can carry on. He heard it, can you not hear it too? The car is approaching. Coming along, coming at you, and yes, me too. Coming from somewhere around the corner and coming now into view. Encroaching on everybody else, but you. Did you know that you can actually hear a car coming around the corner for miles before seeing it over there in a mountainous tropical country style and topic, though? Yeah, the roads are winding over there and for the most part, slow and quiet, among other such things on the diet. Would you like to hear some more about that plan? Well, I'll sell it to you as I bought it from him, yes, from the man. Now let's roll along. Heard that the roads over there were imported and brought in from the

DAY EIGHTEEN

motherland fair. Only upon their arrival there in those tropical spheres did they notice that the roads were much too long for the gear. So, you know they would have to come up with another plan, and they did. Just bend and fold them and place them wherever they can hold them on the skid. That's the one they were to decide upon with ease. So, that was what they did, and now. Those are the winding roads with which the people have to live and plow. Walk the road, and carry the load somehow. Anyhow, and anyway. Back to the story now, of the day. Yeah, as said before, wordplay is the order of the day around here.

19

Look at This, Not That

He heard it, listened, and the vehicle was approaching. Sit, sit back down, and be quiet, good. Now watch this carefully. "I'm glued." The vehicle is still coming, it's winding around the corner, and humming. He's got to get out of sight and quickly, so... After hearing the vehicle approaching, though. Look at him go. That's how it has been with him ever since he took to that stick he's been carrying. It had become the norm for him to stay away from people and their inquiring stares, from the inside of their vehicle, always. From the multitude of questions and those comments of theirs, those very people over there in the hallways. No, no, don't do that; you must stay focused on the motoring track. Look ahead of... I mean. Keep on looking, we don't want you to miss a thing, see? It's not hard this time. He's got enough time to get out of sight and to get thee behind him, yes, Satan, like, the best ratings. Behind that tree, too, that one right there, even. No escaping now, *good evening*. Well, none for the tree. But as for him? That's going to be quite another thing. He's staying put behind the tree there and is well stationed. It's big enough to keep him concealed and covered up, too. If he's careful to wrap himself around the queue, you know, like, sliding around the trunk of the tree as the vehicle gets closer to thee. While using the backside of the said tree to hide in the process, and hence. Changing the angles to stay out of sight and aligned with the blindside of them. It's coming on still, can you not see the light ascending the hill? But then, what's this I now see, coming in? Oh no, here comes the other car, go. Man, oh man, what a bad-luck slam for the prick man. "No!" Now he must go, the car is coming from the other direction, not too slowly, so. Coming from the opposite, by far, in and on the go. Busted, he is going to be unless... "Unless what?" Unless he's to be thinking quickly and critically to get out of this mess. But after all, he's "Prickly," yes, very smart and tall. Got to have a new plan when your plan doesn't work out at all. Or find another one quickly. Bingo. This is Prickly as the thing goes. Now, look at him go. "What's that? What is he doing?" "Wow, look at that, come and get your schooling." Everybody does this at some point or another. There's nothing to it, clever. Cover your eyes, don't do... do. Don't do that. You can't be there staring at the boy like that. Didn't your mama teach you *"nuttn?"* Anything at all? Come on, Guyurl, yes, that would be you, girl. Turn aside a little. Please! "Okay." Thank you, now, you may. You may look, yes, you can look now, "see?"

"No, but but... what did I miss?"

"He was pulling out the pole and pointing. Yes, that's what was happening. He was pointing it up at the base of the tree trunk with the anointing." With one hand holding on to the future, yes, that. The future of all mankind, cuter than just your pops, can't you see? Or at least he's acting the part of the blind, from behind the tree. The other hand was stretching across the face to get a hold of the shirt collar space. Pulling it upright and over his head somewhat. To hide the face you know, from people like him and you, viewing the spots. Look, both vehicles are two, and they're approaching him and you, slowly now, still. Coming down and coming to a screeching, halting stop on the hill. At least one of them has stopped as the occupants are now staring. Inquisitive nobodies they are, interfering. Want to see or to verify if it's really what they think is going on, and what they think that they see. Is that in fact what is going on, or going to be? They were asking even me. "I don't know!" I said to them, but... "Get away from me, you perverted sound-off-a-beach," said he, the same old pole — boy, Prickly. Ain't nothing to see here unless... Unless this is what it's going to be. Unless you want what is graciously coming to you from me. That was when I saw it, look.

"What is that? What is he up to now? What is he doing?"

"One question at a time, man, I'm just a witness, not suing." He was easing himself out, look. Look at the spout. No, don't do that, it will be slack.

"But what, what is that?"

"That's it. Isn't that something?"

"What? What was he doing?"

He was easing himself out from behind the tree. What little was left of him being anywhere behind that tree, that could be said to be there anyway. They got the firing... I mean, the message. They got that message, alright. Look, they're getting their staring faces back on the right side of the tissue, to wipe, in spite. Yes, despite the wetting issue that would be happening on the inside of the vehicle and on their way, to bite... I mean, on the way to where they were going. Going along on their way to go somewhere, probably. That, though, was to their everlasting credit, pardon me. Because now an idea is born, birthed in somebody's mind there and then, in the fields of corn and thyme. He has been dragging around a long pole with him ever since, used for this and other such purposes and reasoning things out all evening.

Yes, you may close up the curtains now. What a mess. Wow! That was a wild ride around that side of the great divide, wasn't it?

20

Day Twenty

Find Me A Place to Live

They arrived in the winter wonderland, way up north near the Canadians... and the Longs, Olivine, and Memrie? Took to the new environment like fish to water, sent out to sea. Some of the time, at least. But this winter Wonderland has got a way of getting very summery some of the time for Memrie, however. He was to find out this and had to adapt quickly or else.... He would have "else" it. Since he couldn't adapt quickly. Yes, that's the reason why he would have done the "else" part, yes, trying to make it fit easily. Splitting the seasons of the year into two halves, as it suited him and to his special needs conditions, spots, Ms Sue Hingh. He loved the winter conditions as well as the opportunities it afforded him, because... He was to become Santa Claus, in-house Santa at the shirt factory, and The Depot, at last. Aloada's shirt Factory is near the depot, and there at the factory is where the other stories would have developed quickly, and to his glory. He avoids the outdoors in the summer, though, avoiding it like a plague foe. But now, there's trouble brewing at the other nosy woman's house and home. "Why?" Because her brother had offered to be the replacement Santa gnome. But then, they would have gotten into talking, just like they'd always done, and all too often. Nothing strange about it, nothing at all to go bug-fit, until she would have gone and said a bit too much, again. "Oh, sheet!" Wrong call, and so came the many attempts at a recall.

"But, but, how come?"

"The word was to get out..."

"Out of somebody's brain?"

"No, out of somebody's throat, and further out through a blabbering mouth." Words were to get said that the prickly pole was the person in the Santa suit for the past several years old... cute, ee?

"Yes."

That was when all hell would have broken loose, "mute." "Me?"

"No, because the brother would have withdrawn the offer." The offer to fall in and be Santa. He was not going to be covering himself over in some clothes that weirdo had been under. Auntie and Grandma had to be the adults there and act smarter. Grandma would have been covering the lids of the ears of the two grandkids there. Kids belonging to her other daughter, whose hands were busily wiping the bib bare. Meanwhile, weary legs were dragging her towards the crib for care. Everybody was readying themselves to prepare to go and drag those two kids away from there. Hauling them fast out of their back-sliding skids. Too late for that, dear Enids, and no. No time for laughter in bids, though fair it might have been. Yet he, that little pickney, did. So, as you already know, those kids had already heard what was said, and so... As it was with the cat and that thing about the backpack? The cat had gone out of the bag, and tried as they may. They were never going to be able to get it out of those rambunctious kids' ears like shots and be able to pacify the two little brats there. A change of plan is now in effect. Well, so I hear, Ms. Evette.

21

Day Twenty-one

A Change Is Going to Come

The annual Christmas dinner was going to have to go away as a slinger. Swinging on over to somewhere else to begin her Christmas work as it occurred, you bet. Yes, go bet your own dinner on that, though, I guess. Lucky Lucy was to be that year, you see, or was she? Now, how lucky was Aunt Lucy to have been the one getting called up for duty? Let's see.

It was to be heard coming on in, the high-pitched screaming. Coming in to fall upon their hearing from up there where it came out of her deep throat and streaming, yes indeed, all the way out of her own place in Sutton on the stream, where she lives and fishes for trout to eat, yes, that's what I mean. Aunt Lucy's Lucea place is always neat, yes, that was where, my dear. It came from up there. You know, the sound? The scream that was to come down? The scary sound was coming from over there and was hastening to hop into our ear from somewhere on the inside of her. Our very own auntie, as it occurs. Aunt Lucy is my mother's sister who lives up in the town of Lucea. Because that wasn't the kind of call that she was expecting at all from her sister. She was supposed to be lucky. But now she's not too sure of that since she would have gotten the call-up for duty. She'll soon be coming in from over there to salute me. But was she happy? Not if one were to have gone by the way of the screams they were about to hear. So it would seem to me, my dear. It seemed to me to bear hysteria hanging on in there. The scream, it sure wasn't the joyous type, you know what I mean? "Like, when it was heard coming in through the pipes?"

"The water pipes?"

"Yes, but, heads up." The boys will need to be there well ahead of time, which she most definitely was not looking forward to, to be kind. But Auntie's nosy neighbor had gone in and spoiled the flavor in the broth with a dash of Larisa flavor, and firmly set it into the sauce by putting it to a simmer with her stirring fork... whatsoever. "Or naught?"

"No, no naught, that wasn't the sort. It was with her big blabbermouth, full and running over with the froth, and much too much-telling of tales and talk of the gossiping sort." Ain't no way they could ever allow the two little brats-of-the-day to be anywhere around those parking lots over there at the depot anytime between now and the Christmas Eve party to play, down at the shirt Depot spot if you ask me. At the factory, too, and some people weren't too amused at that. Faces were to be screwed and screwing, even to the fat. No one wanted to go and spoil things for the rest of them. You know, for all of those anxious other kids, just before Christmas Eve even adorns the cribs. And everybody knew that that was exactly what those two were there itching away to go over there to do, do, and get done, at the gigs.

22

Day Twenty-two

Who Will Be Santa Now?
So now, one thing leads to another, since big brother has dropped out of the way of being Santa, and out of the red suit too, and Grandpa... "No, oh no, that's not going to be the answer. It's not going to happen with our grandpa, so forget about him, not that man, sir. The grandpa thing that you were just thinking is not going to happen." So, someone else has got to be found, and quickly. Who will step up to the plate now and be Prickly? I meant to say, be Santa and go save the rep of Elks' precious city by lamp-outs? They would eventually find such a person. But events and happy ever-after happenings are never that perfect for certain. That type is for the curtain, you know, the show curtain kind, over there at "The Gardens." They would eventually find such a one, though. The only problem with the newfound Santa Claus man was that he was way too big for the gig. Well, not for the gig itself but for the suit in which he must be squeezed. Santa's gloves, too. The whole suit and the boots were way too small for his "Foots..." you know. The footy feet thing that he wears in his shoes to cover a tall toe, but that wasn't all that was too small to fit him, no. There was way too little of the other thing to call. Things that they were mightily lacking in the hall. Like, things to put in and make out of the stew, and like... Other things they were left with having to come to grips with anew. Not just the suitcase kit. Yes, that would have been in the lock and locking things up the back too, too quickly. But there was more lacking in other popping things, such as time, way too little of that rhyming kind. Hardly

any time was left for them to go out and find it, and get a new one in, in a good state of mind to find him. Like, for them to go find a new suit or new pants. So you know what is going to have to happen next to you, right, Aunt?

23

Day Twenty-three

Can't You See I'm Busy?
   Mrs. Olivine Long is a very caring, capable, and attentive woman, very busy she has become, too. Like, always busily making plans and gastronomical pots of stew in the hallways. Ever since Christmas Eve, when she started noticing the changes in the kids, and in me, and you. Well, it was just in her own son's sleeves at first, and then came the others. Other people's kids, like yours. Man, it's like she was cursed as it occurred, so it would seem. But she herself has changed somewhat since then. She has become a lot like... like a lot more domesticated cat, my friend. Washing and baking, and the messy plating. Mopping, dusting, cleaning, brushing, planning, and leaning. Leaning on the everlasting arm of Hingh. Whilst the other arm is not pretending to be elbow-propping up her own chin, sometimes. Banging too, banging pots and pans anew. And you?

   Meanwhile, look at that child, Memrie is a whole lot more reclusive, and not without still being reasonably active. To add to the already overly sensitive self-esteem issue with his skin, keying in, and as it pertains to all those things with his condition, seasonings. He has now gone and frozen the skin off his "sin Ting" Jamaican Grapefruit drink from the sun tanning. Yes, that thing that was handed down to him from his father to his son in the planning. Now it's the man who has made a life out of covering up from toe to sight, even on the inside of his condo at night. That same someone can — "Oh no, he cannot."

DAY TWENTY-THREE – | 55 |

"Well, I must agree." He can hardly bear to cover himself with anything below the pod. Other than for the cover of darkness, soft and slow. "Oh gosh, my god, no."

"What, what was that?"

"Nothing." And of the night.

"Oh no, that can never be right."

So, he stays locked away in a tiny room, tight, and out of people's staring sight. Hoping and praying for his healing rites. Hoping it will come someday, soon, very soon someday. Preferably by the next moon, on Monday, I'd say. He never looked at him, as in, at himself. Has never peeped in through the wonders of the mirror there to delve. He stays away from it as if it were biting teeth, like a dog's, probably. Or something sweet to avoid the diabetes cause — "Hippadidoodah, pardon me." He avoids it like the plague, but... but nowadays. His mother has promptly chandeliered her way in. She's been working hard on a surprise for him, come this Christmas week to begin, and it's all but done. There will be a mirror, mirror on the bathroom wall, as of this early Christmas morning call, yeah, that soon. From the night of Christmas Eve to be pleased. A camera, too, will be hiding out somewhere and hidden away from his view, a surprise it is to be, too. Probably somewhere in the ceiling, to hide the healing in the summer winds feeling. Wouldn't want it to be too revealing. You know, like. To be too peeling and peeping away at him. Just an information-gathering device for one purpose only, for monitoring the vice. Oh, the wisdom of her latest ideas, Homey, a mother's advice. Nothing more, nothing less. "Nice, eh?" "Well, I guess."

24

Day Twenty-four

The Spies' Eyes

She would have had some help from her friends, at best. Helping her in getting the camera and the lens in... as in, *invest*. He would have invested it in them and their schemes and recorded something. Or, just to install it up there near the attic.

If prickly pole should panic or act in any way like a vomit, oh goddamn it. Like, like in a way, unnaturally frightening. That mirror will be out of that place before one can say; mirror, mirror, get off the wall, clear. Or even happy New Year. But there would have been no need for that at all because Prick would have taken to it like...

"...like what? Like a rabbit?"

"No," it was rather slow and amusing at first, like this, as seen from the sightings on the video machine purse when the two spies had eased into opening it up worse and had gotten to the review. "*Seit dey.*" Now, look at it. And begin the discussion, discussing, and stop being that disgusting.

He shook himself awake and looked around the place. It was probably due to the musky smell of the rain coming down the eavesdropping drain, in haste. The one that had come calling to saturate the bright golden sunshine from the early morning with the rain, in this case. Fell flat out there on the hot, sun-drenched ground without a warning again. As loud as the stinky smell of a shaggy dog tail wet and browning, my friend. Now that he's up and wide awake, though. Might as well go and get a shower, fake show. If he... Cain or Abel. Like. If he is able to manage things and hobble along, still dragging the stick with him to the pan. But the two spies were to pick up the stored story's eyes somewhere around this point, when they were reviewing the tape later for the gory... as in, details. Well, "Oink!" Yes, Ms. Piggy, one of them did at first. The other couldn't bring herself to look at the curse.

"You go on, guyurl, you can take the plunge in -I can't look at that."

"Yes, you can, yes you can. You can do it, you and me, together. After all, we are in this together, no?"

"No, no. You go on, go."

Miss Nosy Neighbor prompted. But Mrs. Long was adamant that she didn't want any part of that aspect of the spies' eyes on the kid. She wasn't planning on looking at the Long Man's plan. So. Here he comes, the prickly one.

"Note from the author."

Just a note of "thank you" to say, thanks for choosing to read my book and for sticking with the story thus far. You must be liking it an awful lot, my star. At this point, I want to thank you very much for your patronage and to ask you, my reader, please, take a minute or two to post a review of the book on the Sales pages at Barnes and Noble, Amazon, Kobo, and any other such sales pages, or wherever you might have bought it. This small gesture is so very important to me and very much appreciated. Don't keep it to yourself as they did; be sure to share this. Thank you.

25

Day Five

Seeit Yah Now, Look At It

He followed the door into the bathroom, slowly. Head forward over the hunched frame of the body, half-mooned to "floor" me, almost still snoring. Legs pretending as if they were not at odds with one another. Staying apart, and bent bowed sideways at the knees, on the brother. Well, that was as seen from the point at which the legs were to begin to become most revealing to the thieves. Then down from there to the bed-slippers that were dragging the feet along the floor below the ceiling. Above those slippers were the bedsheets he had wrapped around his waist and held in a bundle somewhere around the navel area case, to unpeel him. The effort would have served to protect the bare essential areas, but there were a couple of instances when the jewelry was threatening to spill through the cracks in the trinket box and hear us, as they were about to fall through the V-shaped opening, and out. Sliding down and away generously below the knees, but the difference in the bathroom was to strike him plumb in the gaze up at the moon when he would have sneezed and flicked the switch alight. There were enough residual lights from the outside flooding in through the window that night. Enough for the spy to have been able to see up to this point, before the gut busts came bursting into the joint. Now, look at that. He stopped abruptly in his tracks and stared at the place where the wallpaper used to be. He saw himself in that very place, looking back at him to see... speaking of "back," that was what was to follow next, one two three steps back to a staggering and then stop he would. To slowly go pick up his jawbone from where it had dropped him — "Good." Then, he turned and looked around the place and behind the door, even. Then up at the ceiling rather slowly, too, to see who might have been leaving. This was to get the spying, nosy neighbor a backward jolt of her very own, from you. For one brief moment there, she thought he would see the camera and "out" their plan, but no, not so. "Now, c'mon." Prickly nimbly walked up closer to the place. Stood in front of the washbasin and stared at himself in the mirror, yes, that space. Then slowly turned around to examine more and more of the strange things that he was seeing, like. His face atop his own body, as if for the first time, in greetings. But not to be that strange anymore after this evening, and on through the night. "Probably." Yes, that would be sweet, Hing, and Addie-lee. The viewing would have ended quite abruptly when he died, I mean, when he did it. It happened when he took both corners of the bedsheets with either hand. Up at the point where it was held together in front of him in a bundle before the man, and slowly began to ease it open to look at the...

"Whoa!" she exclaimed, with a gigantic scream I couldn't explain. She flipped the lid on the laptop closed and stumbled backward with both hands covering her mouth. In an apparent attempt at stuffing the screams back inside and stopping the "out," but... It's too late for that now, and mammy Veenie would have been quick with a pair of supporting arms around her nip... I mean, her hip, somewhere below the neck of the cow. "It's alright, dear," she said, It's alright. Relax. She almost could not, because she almost got to see more of the Prick man in the box than she wanted to before that day should come, which is just about readying itself to get to the come, according to the look of developmental things now happening around the Long Man's home. Yeah, man. That's how we were able to overcome, Jamaican yawdy SinTing, again.

26

Day Twenty-six

Cover Me, Oh! Cover Me

Before those times, like in the past, the mirror on the wall in the bathroom was covered over with paper walls and all. Wallpaper, yes, Mister Hall Tater; an effort at securing the young man's vapor. As well as his sanity, if only a bit safer. Olivine would have kept a large stand-up mirror in her own room, along with others installed in furniture; for her own personal use, mi sure. Yes, I'm quite sure of that, mi goon. But as for her son, he would have none, up until *nung*. Yeah, even now, that's a better word. Up to this point in time. So, *goh siddung*, nerd, no? Go over there and sit. Go sit on it.

As part of the Christmas preparation. Mrs. Long would have cleaned up the mirror and removed all of the old, ugly wallpaper. In the place of the papers, she placed a huge bath towel to cover it, starting right about where the face was. "Oh, sheet!" She didn't want to assault the young man's visions too abruptly in derision, with it. He would surely see the changes in the cubicle, she knew it. But it would be left up to him to decide whether to proceed further in, to spew it. He was given the choice of whether or not to follow through and pursue it, and take the plunge long-wise. Killing him softly, she was… You know what I mean, right? Nice. Now. The hour has come, look. He followed the door into the tiny bathroom; actually, he would have come out of one tiny room just to get into the other. Everything around and about him was tiny by then, except for… "Holy haven, what's that?"

"Oh, never mind, just kids, kids, and more kids, yes, and the cat. Those kids again, one of a kind little brat on the lot, is what they are. Look, they're in the room there, and in earshot to remain. Look at them running out again to get into the hall, and back out again."

27

Day Twenty-seven

Help Me, Please!
   A woman's work is never done, as was said before those times and on, so they say to someone. So, she had to help them out in some way with the Christmas plan. Mrs. Long had to be making herself busy helping them out with the Santa suit, too. Not the boot, though, couldn't help with that foot on the toe. "True." She never blinked an eyelid, it would seem, not as early as I did, at least. I mean, as one task was done, it was on to the next one, like, on to another scene. She had to work the hem and back seam, trying to let out any and all of the extra space she could find in the Santa suit kind of thing. From the waist, at the back, and down to the cuff, at that. At the foot, too, or the hem if that's what you so choose to call them, buff. "Oh, gosh." Or you can just go ahead and deal him a bluff. And yet, when that was found not to be quite enough, she had to add more patches of red and white to the crotches. To the waist and cuff stripes, too, all of those mismatches. Santa was rather eccentric last Christmas Eve night, and yet, a little child shall lead them right, or wrong. Even now, she's leading you along, yes, you, Mr. Man. Who knew? As the saying goes again. When no one else will walk the board, leave it all up to the child; there it goes. Yes, there goes your closely guarded secret load, gone a mile up the road, or down. A child always seems to know where the feeling goes. Going around— "Where's Santa—the real Santa?" She was heard asking this straight-faced, and sitting there on Santa... aah, somebody's knee. In the place where the real Santa used to sit, and should have been, in the present

schemes of Santa's kinds of things, but it was not him. She knew more about Santa than all of them put together there (as it would have seemed to appear). Definitely more than any of them gathered there would have wanted a child to know on Christmas Eve. Or just before the breaking and entering of the thieves. And yes, you know, like, more than they would have wanted her to know any at all, while still being a child, and small. She knew that Santa was short, not tall. At least he's shorter than this one. "This man here, look at him, he most certainly is not Santa."

"Oh, dear! Who then, who's he, who's that imposter sitting there behind his knees? Can someone tell me, please?"

She knew that Santa didn't wear a watch. Like, like this one, and the only person who wears a watch like this is Mister pwòooahhh — "No, baby, you shouldn't say that." But in all of that, the knowledge of facts surrounding the things that the kiddo knew a lot about, she also knew that Prickly...

Now she will have to bite through her grandma's palm quickly if she's ever going to finish the yawn and go on saying what everybody knew she was about to say. Yay. It really did happen that way, no child's play.

28

Day Twenty-eight

Let's Go Back, Way Back
   Back to Memrie and Olivine Long, mother and son. But how did things ever get to be this messy for everyone, anyway? Here for you is the replay and the "Prickly song" of the day. Well, probably.

Mr. Prickly, Prickly pole that is, would have reached out and grabbed hold of the first and closest piece of "long thing" that was to come across him. Can you see it clearly from there? Okay, keep on looking, but don't stare, you'll still see. If you can't quite see, just wait a minute to be. You'll soon be hearing it from someone else, but who is she? Sure, not me. It was a pole, a metal pole, he would have stuck it straight up in front of him, in the hold. Straight and steady. Then pull out and place the ever-ready... Well, not quite, not tonight. It was never always ready to put up a fight, but let's say, to be in the right, let's just say — the other pole, the short pole. He placed it behind the other one. The short one behind the long one, and between himself and the said piece of metal, lead, thing, to carry him along on the polly plan. Relieved he was to become, because he got it all right, or more like, "lost it" all night. He would have lost it. Look, all of it is right there, like his last kick, from last year. While ahing away under his breath to stay, fully rid of air. Felt sooo... good.

At the same time, he, the other guy. Mr. Stranger Cowardly can't lie. He was coming, approaching the intersection, coming in from the opposite direction. He saw him coming, the Prickly one did. Or did he? Let's see, or more like. Let's hear what he has to say about this mystery, as he's there now, retelling the tale to somebody. "I could have sworn I saw him walking towards me, coming. Approaching from the opposite direction. It seemed to me as if he was humming a song or something, perhaps to get our attention. (Obviously) I was wrong," said the man, "I was mistaken."

The whole thing was rather perplexing, so said he, to them; still, there, listening to him. It was made obvious to somebody that the guy was working. He was just there doing his thing. He's a surveyor and was there holding up the pole stayer for his partner player. I was scratching my head and wondering while turning around to look, scanning the entire area. To the left, and then to the right, and scratching yet again, as if I were a fool and not too bright. I'm still a bit confused tonight, but where is the other one? Where is his partner, his friend in the plan? If that is really as it was to appear from where I stand? I was questioning myself for an answer to see the man. Usually, there are always two of them when they are doing the surveying thing for me. One for the pole and the other with the real machines or any such other means of equipment for her role. Of rolling her around the ring, is what I mean, like the camera. Or whatever it is that those people use to get the job done to hammer her, until tomorrow. In the evening, even. I looked around again, and behind me. I knew he must be there somewhere. But where? (Remind me). I couldn't quite see, I was wondering! And then again, I was pondering hard about what I would have been likely to see. But then...

"No, oh no, it can't be." Those words were to be heard coming out of me. "But why was he behaving like that, P?" the man shot back at me. Why was that strange look on his facial attack to see? Was I missing something there? He had to have asked and stared. Well, not anymore, my dear. Not from that point on, he said, I'd sworn swear.

The camera was hanging on my shoulder before, he continued. Hanging on by the long string, yes, but not anymore. I started out preparing to do something. Like, to work, even. Capturing whatever I could of whatever it was that might have been going on there, in the hood. Or not going on. I couldn't afford to miss that one, you know.

DAY TWENTY-EIGHT

If it's something, like I thought it might be, I had to capture it, "To show it off to the kids," I'd said, if nothing else, to put in bids for me, but... Look, look at it now, here's the evidence. I wanted to capture it all, you know. See? It's all here on the recording reel for the recall, as we are here now reviewing it, and sitting in the hall. Look. Focusing now, and shooting, that's me there, recording it all. No looting.

Meanwhile, look, look at that, Jonny P, yes, he, him. John Public and everybody else were passing by me and seeing these things, by way of the careless eye, links you know. But not necessarily because they were looking. My, oh my, Hingh. Must have been thinking the very same thing as I was at the beginning. "It's just a couple of surveyors going about their business. Doing the job a favor in the evenings." One of them is holding up the pole, straight and steady, and the other is shooting the job... already. Or no, capturing is the proper thing to be saying. On the go, and swaying. I was the other person there with a camera, capturing the scenes for sure. But Mister Man, the prickly poley one, it was he who was there holding up the pole and shooting too. All in the hidden one's view. Who knew? All those things were seen happening down there on the corner near the Aloada Shirt Factory, but. "Look at what I've got now, waiting to talk to somebody about the fee." Here comes that Prickly Poles' song again. Wait for it, wait for it.

29

Day Twenty-nine

The End Is Coming. Of the World, Even, It's Got to Be Look, look at them, the two of them are there, walking side by side along the bustling sidewalk, my friend.

"Where?"

"There." They're going towards the diner there on the corner. Yeah, that's them right there. They're getting really tight of late. Tighter than the hinged door is when bolted on and locked down on the gate. It's a new day in a new year, so I hear. Well, it's not really all that new a year anymore, it's coming on down close to Saint Valentine's door, sorry, I meant to say, day. Saint Valentine's Day, and the old boy Prickly is starting to learn how to play. Look at them, going away again. She has fixed him, sorry again, I meant to say, she's fixing him up properly again today, look, look, look at them. She's pulling up his collar now, after she was done pulling down on the hood. Trying to settle it in on the tunic, good. He still has this tendency of wanting to cover up his face when out in a public space, you know, not good. Because there really is no further need for that at all, he has finally cleared up the pole off the skin wall, and all that "mole-like spoke" that used to make one's skin crawl... well. Not quite "all," not all of the moles, not all of them are gone. It wasn't really him at that, either, who had done it. The heavy lifting is off it, and it's definitely not gone out of his mind; obviously, he is still trying hard at hiding the signs, goddammit. Signs that are still tattooed onto his mind, but she won't let him. Not this time. She might get some other things to fit upon him, though, well, maybe, but.

DAY TWENTY-NINE

It's going to take him quite a long time, it would seem, to come to terms with the idea that he has now got skin as normal as anybody else's gal, nice and clean. All around town, like that one hanging on the arm, my pal, even. Tall and brown. Her new job around these paths now is to vet and pet him, and...

"And what?"

"...and you know, like, try and see if she can get him to want to get into her..." You know? Like, get into the idea that they really are a unit now. That they can go out, or even come in. They can go and plow anywhere, and anytime they like, now, and like, want! The fields, that is, we are talking about the fields that they're planning on planting here, you know. So, as is the norm in those things, to go, they can now go out and plow the fields and plant the seeds, and plan them too, to try and preserve the breeds. Well, the seeds may well have been planted already, come to think of it. Since summer is just around the corner, as is the normal habit. As you already know, one should not wait until the very last minute to date... Or to get the seeds into the ground to grow when it's warmer. Otherwise, one runs the risk of being late as a farmer, or getting left behind at the starting gate with not much to put on the plate to storm her. Nobody wants to make that mistake, like Ms. Warner. Certainly not her; not Miss Nosy Neighborly, his date. No, wait. As for Mrs. Long, something, I mean, Mistress Olivine Long. As for her? She seems to be really taking a liking to the new condition as it pertains to and applies to both of them. As to how they have been getting along in recent times, to go out and spend on...

30

Day Thirty

Oh My Gosh, Look at Him Now

One could hardly have imagined that the prickly could have come back so quickly from such a place and state as he was forced to walk the stick, Leigh. Or more like, not being able to walk a single bit. "Oh my me!" "Yes, I agree." He could hardly even move. As a matter of fact, no siree. Let alone walk the block, towards me. He was made to just lie there upon the stalk. Sorry, I meant to say, upon the sticky sickbed cot. Upon that pole thing, he was forced to drag in upon it as said...

"What, upon what? Upon his head?"

"No," not really on his head, but, you know, upon him. No, wait a minute, not that either, it was he who was upon the darned thing. But that was then, this is now. "Oh. Look, look at that cow."

"Look at what cow, where is it?"

"Look at that cow, yes, that's what I said, no, wait. You're a bit late if you didn't see the plate." But I've got a feeling that you only need to wait; you are bound to see him do it again, not too much later down the interstate, my friend. He was tugging at the hood again, trying to pull it up over his brain, but she won't let him. Not while these good times remain. Would have slapped him on the backside of the Palm kind of things, yes. She's been wanting to slap it, you know, the habit. She wanted to slap it from last week, it would seem, clear out of him, like a dream. It has now begun to become the norm for her to reform him, and then try to storm him with the winter wonders of heart corn things. Like, those that are already planned by her for him, in her haunted red water, pumping something there in her upper chest frame, for a Long hill's name. But Santa was pleased last Christmas Eve. Would have gotten down on his knees to work on the beads after he was done picking the fruity pods off the trees. "Or was, was, wasn't it off the sticky beads on the trunk of the tree stick thing? "Oh, yeah, I forgot about him. It was that, yes, a pole." A metal pole of some sort was attached to the spot, over the wart. Which would have been way too cold to accommodate the whole thing, without having it all fall out of control, and cause him to sin. So, the saintly old grandpa, that same old Nicholas Santa. Would have wandered in and entered the prickly pole-ish chamber, along with a whole bunch of his helpers. While his mother was slumbering there under the dreaded sounds of thunder, shaking scared in her rooming shelter. Santa and friends were to perform miracles and wonders, again. So now, just as things were in the days of the former, as it applied to prickly and his Polish blunder. Some things are just about to get going, going, gone. Like, gone away, again, and here comes that annoying prickly pole song again. Or the updated version of the same.

Oh boy, Prickly, Prickly prickly pole, poor boy prickly, prickly Prickly pole. Got himself, got himself, got himself stuck to a pole, stuck to a cold old metal pole. It's cold out on Christmas Eve.

Oh boy, prickly Prickly Prickly pole, poor boy prickly prickly Prickly pole. Got himself, got himself, got himself stuck to a pole, stuck on a cold, old metal pole. He's whole on Christmas morning.

Come, one fairy whose palm was hairy. Sliding down through the mirror since there was no home chimney –*scary*, but when he woke up next. His mom was in the room, *as usual*. With the bowl and a spoon —*as usual*— cooking and cleaning from morn till noon —*as usual*— but, but, but again. Woke up whole. Prickly pole, woke up whole. Woke up whole, or was he?

Solo.

It was on a painy Christmas morn, Christmas morn, Christmas morning. He woke up in the Morn... and yawning —*yawning*— Covering his mouth over, and over with his palm, Hingh, *still yawning*. To discover without so much as a warning. The pole is gone, the skin is, Norm, he and his nosey neighborly personality have got something new going on. And now look, he's holding on to his brand-new mom, and...

"What just happened?"

"He fainted," thought he was dead and buried, gone to heaven, and not to his bed carried. Or, someone is about to get married. Him perhaps! Laughs. Hahaha ha ha ha haa. Well, it could have been that you know, or something. But, but. Cut.

Look at them, there they are, going along, passing the car, hand in hand, and then, they were to kiss. For the first time ever, for him at least. If you'd missed it at that time. Here it comes again, the kissing kind, my friend. Can't seem to stop doing it since then. Just like this, look at it. *Hmm-muah*. Yes, that's how the prick was to be kissed and to be discussed. All over and around town. It's a must, again. Amen.

31

Day Thirty-one

Surprise, Surprise

Finally, she would have gotten him to say yes to her; the prick had promised to show her where the big mess occurred. As it turned out, though, the nosey neighbor didn't know all that much after all. Not quite as much as she thought she knew on the first call. Prickly went shopping without her knowing, as she was to find out later that evening. There were more discoveries to be made, too, yeah! Coming her way from over near Discovery Bay and running into you. Man, that boy Prickly is really learning how to play, and he's as strong as an overpriced bull today, called-up and spitting fire as if coming out of a New York City Yankees' bullpen to play, and pulling the win off the Bulls again. The least to say.

They were walking back through the park in a lock, yes man, locking hands up with fingers together like that, after they were done watching "The Attack." You know, the chick flick they went to see at the Cinemax over at the city's movie complex. It was his humble and lowly offering to her on Valentine's Day, sure. But to even up the score, he had for her a little bit of a surprise more. He decided to fill her in on the incident, the metal polemic happening, he meant. He was going to be retracing the steps as they had happened on the fateful day's wet. Now they're in the park and walking past just about where he had picked up the pole thing. Watch the scenes; he's pointing it out to her, the whole thing.

"Look, look, that's the exact spot where I picked it up. The darned thing was cold; I could feel it through the hold on the coffee cup. But the thickness of the gloves didn't quite reveal it enough, so I walked on through the cold. Hurrying to drag my weary legs along, due to the urgency in the bowl. I needed to go, you know, over to the pan. But everywhere I looked, people were on the other go, going about their business... show, man! I had to unload or carry home the load in my clothes; I chose to do the former. I was standing right there on the corner when I decided to fall back onto the thing that had worked for me in the beginning. P-hissing up against the sticky something, I stuck it up. The pole, and then pull it out just like this." Look, look, his hand is now coming out of his pocket, Nook.

"What, what, what are you doing? What are you doing? What is this?" This was to be the real "it." The evening's special gift. Prickly pole went into his pocket and fished out the tiny box of it. Whilst sinking on one knee in front of the town to see. Right there on the corner where he had once stopped to p-p..., goodness gracious me. I'm stuttering again, can't quite call the name. But. He knows full well that he should not be p-p... preaching the gospel on the corner of the street, without first securing a handful of the city's enabling permits. But. Cut.

Nosy is in another world now, and a whirlwind, too. "Wow." She was to be swept up off her feet a moment ago when Prickly didn't hear the word "no" in response to the question he'd posed with his knee down close to his toes, I mean, hers, her toes. Boy, that boy is really strong, look at him carrying her along. What a difference a year can make sometimes. Just over a year ago, this time. The prick was riding around a clothesline. Or some other such thing of the kind. But then, he would have stepped up his game and added a metal pole to his name. But look at him now, his head hunched over the cow. I mean, over Miss Nosy, she who knows nothing how... She's his fiancée now, though, well, I suppose the vow is to be coming soon, somehow. Very soon, too. But as of now? As for me, and you? I don't know, man, but look. Take a sneak peek at this thing and then look through, did you see it? Yes, he's carrying her along like a ballerina dancing man. Walking the same path that he had crossed on a stick stalk that was wedged up near the ask me no more questions about the fund part. I'm almost done with the talk. Now. Look at him, fast, he's carrying her in through the same building door, *Sin Ting*, or something. That was where he had entered before with a metal pole up near the bowl. Grimace and pain on his face, then, so I was told. But now there's joy and laughter in that place, often. Cut the darned thing, the joy's not stopping. They're on the inside now, and prick just kick-closed back the door with the cow still in hand, and…

"Oh, my lord! What do you think is going on there now in the yard?"

"Swallow hard if you want, and stop." It's not your business card to swap. Your business is not anything such as that. So, go sit down over there and relax, then come back over here and face up to the end. Bet you can't put it down without reading it, again!

E Lloyd Kelly is "WritingElk," an Author, poet, and songwriter, sometimes. Born in Jamaica, West Indies, to Raglan and Alma Kelly. Now resides in Montreal, Quebec.

Other works by E Lloyd Kelly include;

• The "Real Inky Trail Series."

• Backsliding. A novel: Chicken soup from heaven for what ails a people.

• Training Manley. Among others.

Find these and more on the Author's page at Amazon.com/author/elloydkelly or here: http://www.amazon.com/-/e/B01G7NYWL6

I'm E Lloyd K, the WritingElk, and I'm out.

This is a copyright-protected work. 2019. By E. Lloyd Kelly. All rights reserved.

www.ingramcontent.com/pod-product-compliance
Lightning Source LLC
Chambersburg PA
CBHW072106110526
44590CB00018B/3329